Twitter for Business: A How-To Guide

ISBN: 1-4565-3895-0
ISBN-13: 9781456538958

Twitter for Business: A How-To Guide

Abby Gilmore
VERTICAL MEASURES

Volume Editor: Michael Schwartz
Editorial Coordination by: Elise Redlin-Cook
Designed by: David Gould

2011

Dedication

For my tweeps—the people who have inspired me to write this how-to guide, KFM and my family for putting up with all my Twitter talk, and to the #twibe for making my Twitter experience worthwhile every day. Thank you.

Table of Contents

To Tweet or Not to Tweet

Since Twitter was founded, participation has steadily increased...and it's still increasing every single day. Many think creating a brand presence on Twitter may not be the right thing for their business, though that's hardly the case.

First of all, why *not* join Twitter? It is another way to get links to your site, create a buzz about your brand and build connections with customers and other industry professionals.

Still not convinced? Here are a few more reasons:

- Share what you know about your product and your industry with others
- Get traffic to your website
- Help with SEO if messages are optimized
- Get feedback from your customers
- It's fast, free and far-reaching

Throughout this how-to guide, each of the above points will be discussed at length. But first, what exactly is Twitter?

What is Twitter?

Twitter is a micro-blogging website developed by a group of people who worked at the podcasting company Odeo, Inc. in South Park, a small neighborhood in San Francisco. Since its creation in March 2006, Twitter has become an Internet phenomenon, with more than one hundred million users. People use Twitter for a number of reasons—to talk with friends, connect with strangers and to relate to brands they love...and that's where you come in.

Twitter enables its users to send short, 140-character messages, which are displayed on the user's profile page. By default, Twitter profiles are public, which means anyone can see the messages displayed on a user's profile page. You can protect your tweets by making them private; however, if the profile is set up for a brand it should be public. Public tweets can show up in search engine results, while private tweets will not.

Users can subscribe to other users' profiles and tweets by "following" them. Once you follow someone, the tweets that user sends will show up on your home page, and vice versa. Twitter also enables people to talk directly to other users by "@replying" them, or by direct messaging them. While, @replies are public, direct messages are private.

Users can send and receive tweets via Twitter.com, as well as a number of third-party applications on the web. Users can also tweet through SMS text messages or third-party Smartphone applications. Twitter is free, though standard text messaging rates apply for SMS Twitter use. Additionally, users can upload pictures and videos to applications and then post the hyperlink in a tweet.

Is there a place for me on Twitter?

Quite simply…the answer is, YES! There is a place for almost everyone and every brand on Twitter. Don't believe me? Head to Twitter.com to see for yourself.

Once on the Twitter website, you will see the search box, like this:

Simply type your brand name in the box and click search. You will see real-time tweets mentioning your brand name.

If you don't see any results for your brand name, try searching one of your product or service names or a competitor's brand name. In the case of Vertical Measures, let's try link building services.

Chances are people are talking about your business or your industry on Twitter. If your brand is not on Twitter, who is going to engage these people? That's right…your competitor.

So, how does Twitter make a social media marketing plan complete?

When you think social media marketing, the big players are Facebook, Twitter, YouTube and LinkedIn. These sites allow you to provide content to your audience, which is key when it comes to marketing.

Twitter is an information sharing platform, according to Kevin Thau, Twitter's Vice President for business and corporate development. "Twitter is for news. Twitter is for content. Twitter is for information," he said.

Therefore, Twitter is the perfect platform to use to share information with your customers or potential customers. It is a way to reach out to people unhappy with your brand or service. It is a way to reward loyal customers. Though you may think you can do this on any social media platform, Twitter is the champion. Since most of the information posted on Twitter is available to the public, it serves as the best way to talk to customers one-on-one via social media.

If you choose not to utilize Twitter in your social media plan, you will forfeit access to valuable information such as vital insight into your prospects and customers as well as possible leads and conversions.

In a recent study by Chadwick Martin Bailey, a custom market research and consulting firm, researchers found that consumers who are fans and followers of brands on Facebook and Twitter, respectively, are more likely to recommend or buy from that brand.

The study goes on to explain "60 percent of Facebook fans and 79 percent of Twitter followers are more likely to recommend those brands since becoming a fan or follower. And an impressive 51 percent of Facebook fans and 67 percent of Twitter followers are more likely to buy the brands they follow or are a fan of." [1]

In summary, social media can directly impact your sales if you take it seriously. So, what are you waiting for?

How Twitter fits into Internet Marketing

Twitter is only one piece of a social media plan, and social media is only an aspect of an Internet marketing strategy. And believe it or not, there is more to social media than Twitter and Facebook.

Other social media sites to consider:
- Your blog. Hopefully your blog is hosted on your site, if you have one (which you should!). Your blog is a place to publish content that anyone can leave a comment on, as well as provide your own opinions, research and findings on hot topics surrounding your industry, while doubling as a community for visitors. Often times, you will promote this content through other channels like Twitter and Facebook. It has been said before and I'll say it again—content is king. Good content is essential in being successful in the social media realm.
- YouTube.com. YouTube is a website where you can to upload and publish videos and host them on your own channel. You may think you aren't in the industry where videos would be useful, but you would be surprised. Think about creating videos to aid customers in decisions about your brand or product, or perhaps just to demonstrate your product and how it works. Maybe an interview series with industry experts would be beneficial for your target audience. If you publish quality video content and optimize it, it is another way to draw in customers.
- Slideshare.com. Do you present slideshows at presentations? Do you create slideshows for webinars? Can any of your blog posts be repurposed into slideshows? If so, upload those slideshows onto Slideshare.com, a site that lets you share presentations with others.
- Niche social media sites. In almost every industry, there are a number of niche social media sites, specific to that subject. These sites are where people who work in or are interested in your industry will be, so it is essential to be active on these platforms.

How social media fits into Internet Marketing

Link Building

As mentioned before, social media is one facet of an Internet marketing plan. How does it fit into the scheme of things? If you are looking to build links for your website, social media is definitely helpful in that aspect. Though some social links are no-follow (which means a piece of code is telling search engines not to follow these links), some in the industry believe these links do actually count for something—especially when it comes to social media. In fact, representatives from both Bing and Google admitted that social signals are used in search engine rankings.

In a recent interview with people from Google and Bing, representatives from both search engines told SEO expert Danny Sullivan[2] "who you are as a person on Twitter can impact how well a page does in regular web search. Authoritative people on Twitter lend their authority to pages they tweet."

And it goes back to the no-follow debate. Representatives from both search engines said that even though tweets are tagged as no-follow, data from tweets are taken into account in certain circumstances. Therefore, your social profiles must be optimized to the fullest extent and your authority must be built up in order to help your link building efforts. Though it is not certain exactly how much a link from Twitter is worth, major search engine representatives are saying that tweets definitely do count for something,

Traffic

If nothing else, participation in social media can bring traffic back to your website. By promoting content placed on your website through social channels, you are ultimately driving traffic back to your website. By building up your authority on Twitter and other social sites and optimizing your profiles, your chances of an increase in traffic boost significantly.

Online Reputation

When your brand name is searched for in a search engine, most likely your website and social profiles will be on the first page, if your profiles are active and well optimized. A company's worst nightmare would be for negative reviews or reports to show up on the first few pages of a search engine, which could deter traffic and customers. To keep your social profiles at the top of your search results, stay active. The more active you are the better—not only for rankings, but also for your audience. Also, the better optimized and keyword-rich your profiles are, the more likely they will appear higher in search engine rankings.

The Nitty-Gritty

Setting up an account is the first step to creating your brand's Twitter profile. But, there are many terms used on Twitter that you must be aware of before you dive in. Here is a glossary to get you started.

Learn the Lingo

Tweet: A tweet is a message you send out to the Twitter world. It must be 140 characters or less.

@reply: When you want to reply directly to someone's tweet, you click the reply button and it will show up in their "mentions" stream.

Retweet: When you see something that you think your followers would like, you can click the retweet button and it will be sent to your followers while citing the original source.

Follow: When you follow someone, you are subscribing to his or her tweets. Tweets that they send will show up in your home feed. To follow someone, go to their profile and click the "Follow" button.

Unfollow: Unfollowing someone would unsubscribe you to their tweets. To do this, go to their profile and click:

Then this menu will appear:

Simply click "unfollow."

Direct Message: If you would like to send a Twitter user a private message, you may do so by direct messaging that person. To do so, go to "direct messages" on the right hand menu. Then you will see this form:

Send ▾ a direct message.   140

send

Choose the follower from the drop-down menu, then write and send your message.

An easier option is adding "d" to your tweet before sending it to any user that is following you. Adding the "d" will tell Twitter to treat the tweet as a direct message.

The person must be following you in order to send a direct message, for spam purposes.

#Hashtag: Hashtags add tweets to a category. Hashtags are just adding the "#" symbol preceding any word. Some popular hashtags are: #followfriday #ff or #musicmonday. Some people just add #tags to words they are using, in order for those terms to be searchable.

For example, if you tag your tweet as #sale, when someone searches "sale," any tweet with "#sale" it will come up. Anyone who does a search for the hashtag you use may find your tweet. Also, if someone sees a tweet in their stream with the hashtag #sale, when they click on the tag, they will be brought to a live feed of any tweet posted that includes that word. For example, this tweet sent by Vertical Measures (@VerticalMeasure) was tagged #SEO. When people search Twitter for #SEO related tweets, this will come up.

#SEO 25 Guest Blogging Resources – Want to be a guest blogger on a powerful blog in your niche? Here are 25 blogs t... http://ht.ly/1932uc
7:24 AM Sep 17th via HootSuite

At Vertical Measures, we frequently tag our blog posts with #SEO as the information pertains to the SEO industry. That way if someone is looking for material related to SEO, our post will show up in search results.

Account Set-Up

To set up your account, you must first think of your Twitter handle, or what name will be associated with your profile and tweets.

The best choice would be your brand name. Obviously, using your brand name as your Twitter handle will make it easier for people to find your profile when searching on Twitter or on the web. But, reserving your brand name as your Twitter handle is also important for brand protection purposes.

People are able to choose whatever Twitter handle they wish, no matter who they are, meaning anyone could register for Twitter using your brand name. This could be detrimental to your brand as someone could impersonate a company representative and say whatever they want. As a result, is it extremely important to reserve your brand name as your Twitter handle as soon as possible.

Now, depending on your brand name, it may already be taken, with more than 100 million registered users on Twitter. If your brand has a nickname or an acronym, that could work, too. But, it must be something that consumers will recognize, or it will be a lot harder to build brand acknowledgment on Twitter.

Your handle should also be short enough to be retweetable, or quotable. If your handle has the maximum amount of characters, others will use up many of their allotted 140 characters including your handle when they retweet your tweets.

Once you have an idea for a Twitter handle (and a backup, in case it is taken!) you are ready for the next step.

Go to Twitter.com in your web browser and click sign up.

Once you click sign up, you will be directed to a page where you fill out your account information.

Consider the "name" field on your profile that is displayed adjacent to your username. This does not have to be the same as your brand name, but typically is. Think about your "name" closely, as it is constantly being indexed by search engines.

Once you are signed up, you must confirm your account through your e-mail address. When you have confirmed your account, you should begin to fill out your profile information.

Once logged in, choose "Settings" from the top right menu.

In the "Account" section, you want to make sure that your Twitter privacy is set to public, by leaving the "Protect My Tweets" box unchecked.

*If you check this box, people who are not following you will not be able to see your tweets, nor will your tweets show up in search engine results.

Next, choose the "Profile" option. This is where you will choose the photo that will be associated with your Twitter account, as well as fill out your bio.

Photo: Your photo should be your brand logo or something recognizable that resonates with your brand. The picture size should be about 73 by 73 pixels.

Name: Brand name.

Location: If you have a physical location for your headquarters or business, add the city and state as your location.

Web: Link to your website or blog. If you don't do this, you are missing out on a free link! Also, it gives people a point of reference—another place on the web to visit for more information.

Bio: You only have 160 characters to describe your brand, so make it good! To write a bio that will attract followers, consider adding some personality. Make your bio relatable. Make sure to get the most important information in there first, like what you do or what product the Twitter profile is representing. Also, you will want to add a keyword phrase associated with your business or product to describe your company, for SEO purposes.

Customization

Customizing your Twitter profile page is very important, as it is another source of branding. Professionalism on the Internet is crucial, as your reputation will follow you. If you are using Twitter to brand your business online, you must have a custom Twitter presence.

The most important element of customization is your Twitter background. If you have a company graphic designer, creating a Twitter background should be a piece of cake. And if you don't, you shouldn't fret, as there are many websites to aid in this process, like MyTweetSpace (http://www.mytweetspace.com/), TwitterBacks (http://twitterbacks.com/) and TwitBacks (http://www.twitbacks.com/).

Your Twitter background should be at least 1280 by 1024 pixels in size, though you can go bigger. Some recommend the background to be 1600 by 1200 and even 2048 by 1600. Though it is unlikely that the majority of your followers will have an extra large computer screen, different size monitors is something to consider. To check out more statistics on the matter, visit http://www.w3schools.com/browsers/browsers_display.asp.

When it comes to colors, it is best to be consistent and make your Twitter page match your website or blog. Again, as your Twitter presence is another part of branding, it is necessary to streamline your efforts. You want to be as familiar as possible to your visitors.

As with everything online, you want to keep the most important information above the fold. Since Twitter background images don't scroll, this is even more important. To be safe, it is recommended to keep your image height around 500 pixels. You should also consider the images you are using. Avoid using images with harsh edges, as this looks amateur.

Continued testing is important when it comes to creating a Twitter background that works. Try out your background in different stages to avoid having to start from scratch. Also, you don't want the formatting to be off. It comes off as unprofessional and to become an authority in your industry, you should be as professional as possible in all endeavors.

Once you have your custom profile ready to go, it is time to start following people and interacting with your followers.

Who to Follow

With millions of people on Twitter, figuring out whom to follow is a daunting task—especially for a new user. Luckily, there are many ways to find people worth following.

One of the most exciting aspects of Twitter to the everyday user is the access to companies and people that they otherwise would not have access to. For example, many celebrities have become extremely active on Twitter. Celebrities see it as a way to directly connect with fans—to speak with them openly and to break their own news to people who truly care.

The same goes for companies—establishments are able to break news to their fans and followers via social media, instead of waiting for traditional news channels to report it. As a result, news agencies are losing their scoop to companies, as they are breaking news before news outlets even know about it. Therefore, it is important to build up your following to be able to connect with people who truly care about your business.

You want to follow people that you could potentially form a relationship or connection with. These people include:

- People in your target demographic
- People talking about your brand
- People interested in your product/industry
- People talking about your competitors
- Icons and experts in your industry

To find these people, it can be as simple as doing a Twitter search for your brand name, competitor's brand name or one of your keywords and seeing who is talking about what, or using Twitter directories or Twitter lists.

For example, if you are in the Internet marketing industry, you will probably want to follow some top names in the field. Also, you will want to follow people interested in the industry, like social media fans, bloggers and SEO lovers. If you do a Twitter search for the keyword "social media" you can find people interested in the topic. You want to follow people in your industry because most likely, some will tweet useful information, links and resources that could be valuable to your followers, and you can retweet this information. You can build connections by retweeting people's tweets, since they will see that you have retweeted them. If they aren't following you but see you have been sharing their tweets with your followers, they may follow you back, especially if you prove to be a resource in the industry.

Though it may seem like a competition for the most followers, it is not the number of followers you have that is important, it is the level of engagement, the spread of tweets you put out and tweets you're mentioned in, level of traffic, swell of links, and overall participation. If you have a million followers but no one is engaging, how useful is that? Not very. With that in mind, once you have a general idea of who you want to follow, you can use the following tools to aid in your search for followers.

Twitter as a Search Engine

Using Twitter as a search engine to find Twitter users is a very easy way to discover followers. If you want to find out if a certain person is on Twitter, you can use Twitter's own account search at https://twitter.com/invitations/find_on_twitter. Twitter's Advanced Search (http://search.twitter.com/advanced) is a tool that is extremely useful when looking for people in a specific industry or people who tweet about certain keywords. Simply fill in the keywords of your choice and Twitter will bring back tweets containing these keywords. You can even include multiple keywords if you are searching for a very specific niche topic.

Twitter Lists

Users set up lists to categorize their followers. For example, some people make a list of people they work with. Others will list people in the same industry, brands they like, funny tweeters, etc. Many users have public lists, so you could look through them if you have an idea of the type of person or company you want to follow. Though this can be slow, it can be beneficial. Listorious (http://listorious.com/) is a search engine that canvases Twitter lists for your search queries. If you search for "comedy," you will get back a bunch of lists that are all related to the subject matter, and so on.

Directories

Twitter users can list themselves in Twitter directories, like Wefollow (http://wefollow.com/). Through Wefollow, you can search by location or topics. If you are looking for users in the SEO industry, search the SEO tag. Users will be shown under two tabs, most influential and most followers.

Other Twitter directories include:
- Twellow (http://www.twellow.com/), which is known as the Twitter Yellow Pages.
- Localtweeps (http://www.localtweeps.com/), which allows you to search by location, which can be useful if you are partaking in local search efforts and want to make connections within your community.
- TweetFind (http://www.tweetfind.com/), which is a general Twitter directory.

Account Management

Once you have your Twitter profile set up, customized and have found a few accounts to follow, you should think about using a third party application to manage your account. There are many free applications that can aid you in managing your Twitter profile easier than managing it via Twitter.com. Many users find it difficult to manage a business account from Twitter.com because of its limitations, like not being able to synch to other social sites or schedule messages.

Using Third-Party Twitter Applications

Tweetdeck (http://www.tweetdeck.com/)

Tweetdeck is a desktop client made just for your social media accounts. You can customize the browser with groups, searches and lists, which will allow you to access information very quickly. This way, you will be able to stay up to date on all the information surrounding your Twitter account. You can also schedule tweets to be sent out at a later time.

Hootsuite (www.hootsuite.com)

Hootsuite is similar to TweetDeck, though you do not have to download it as a desktop client, and you access your account information via Hootsuite.com. Hootsuite is especially helpful if you are managing more than one Twitter account, say for multiple clients. Like Tweetdeck, you are able to customize your experience using lists and saved searches to easily access all the information you need. Scheduling tweets is also very simple in Hootsuite. You can also connect other social media accounts, like Facebook and LinkedIn, for all over the web access through Hootsuite.

Also, with Hootsuite you can invite others to be a part of a certain account. For instance, if more than one person contributes to your Twitter account, you can grant that person access to the account through Hootsuite without ever giving the login and password information. This function makes it easy for more than one person to contribute to an account, as the application tracks which person sends and responds to individual messages. Basic Hootsuite accounts are free, while pro accounts are $5.99 a month and an additional $15 per team member, or person granted access to the account.

CoTweet (www.cotweet.com)

CoTweet is made for business' Twitter accounts and is used by many large companies across the world. The features of CoTweet Standard (the free application) are very similar to Tweetdeck and Hootsuite, as it allows multiple social media platforms to be managed in one place, scheduling tweets, as well as allows multiple users to access each account. If you are a large company and would like to use CoTweet Enterprise, which is specifically designed for larger companies, you may request a demo.

All of these third-party applications do very similar things, so it is up to you to decide what works best for you or your company. I would recommend using all of them and making a decision based on your experience with the individual application.

Linking Social Media Accounts

As mentioned when discussing third-party Twitter applications, many allow you to link up various social media accounts, so you can manage your entire social media presence with one application. This can be beneficial, as all your social media accounts and information can be accessed in one place, though it really depends on what social media platforms you are engaging on. From experience, I have found that many businesses commonly begin their social media marketing implementation with Twitter and Facebook simultaneously.

Linking your Facebook, or other social media profiles like LinkedIn, MySpace or Foursquare, to your Twitter profile via a third-party application can be beneficial, mostly to see all of your information and interactions in one place. Ideally, you will have a different messaging plan for each social media account, since they are targeting different people, so I would not suggest sending the same exact messages across all platforms. However, by linking your accounts to one application, you are able be more timely in your social media interactions. It is much easier to check one application than log in to separate profiles on different platforms constantly throughout the day.

Another social media platform you should not forget about is your blog. Many don't consider a blog to be social media, though it is social media in the truest form. Blogs allow you to share highly accessible information with people while encouraging interaction and participation in the conversation. The key element to consider is disseminating the information through social platforms, which is where your other social media profiles come in.

If you have a blog, a must-do is setting up your Twitter to update through your RSS feed. By doing this, your blog posts are automatically tweeted to your

Twitter account. You can do this by using a third-party application like Twitterfeed (*http://twitterfeed.com/*). Twitterfeed also allows you to send your blog posts to Facebook and other social media sites. Getting this started is pretty simple. Just create an account and follow the four steps to linking your RSS feed to your social media accounts.

With Twitterfeed and other applications like it, you can set the application to check your blog for new updates from every hour to every 12 hours. This will depend on how often your blog is being updated. This tool is extremely beneficial, especially if more than one person is posting to the blog, as you may not necessarily know what time a certain blog post will go live. With a feed service, your account will automatically be updated.

Twitter Lists

I discussed searching other peoples' public Twitter lists earlier to find followers. Setting up your own Twitter lists, both public and private, is essential to Twitter use—especially for a business. As previously mentioned, Twitter lists are groups of people put into different categories. These lists allow you to group like-minded people together and even allow you to secretly spy on your competitors.

Some lists are more useful than others, of course. Comedians or funny people may be great for your personal account, but may be less useful when managing a business Twitter account. A starting point could be setting up a list for the people at your company that have Twitter accounts. That way, you can retweet information they share. In this case, it doesn't matter much if the list is public or private. To create a Twitter list, go to *www.Twitter.com* and sign in. Click "profile" and you will see a navigation bar. Click on "Lists," and a drop down menu will appear, displaying current lists. Click, "create a list," and this box will pop up:

Enter the name of your list. If it's for the company, you could put "Staff" or your company name. Add a description if you want to, though it is not required. Then set the list to public or private. Public lists can show up in searches, while private will not. If you are using a third-party application, adding a stream to your profile will serve the same purpose.

One list that you want to keep private is a list of your competitors. This is a way to follow your competitors without truly "following" them. If you really want to find out your competitors' Twitter tactics, follow all of their employees as well. This stream will serve as a real-time feed of tweets related to your competitors, and will allow you to get a feel for their messaging and overall strategy. Another list that would be beneficial would be experts or icons in your industry. This way, you can keep up with the latest information surrounding your niche.

That being said, Twitter lists can be used as a live stream of information pertaining to a certain subject, too, like one of your keywords. If you are using a third-party application for Twitter management (and like I mentioned, I strongly advise you to look into it if you are using Twitter for business purposes), it is easy to monitor a keyword stream that is set up just like a list. By adding a stream for a keyword or small group of keywords, you can see who is talking about what, all of the time. This information is useful for a number of reasons. First, you are able to monitor what is being said in your niche. Also, you have access to all of these people's thoughts via their tweets. In the next section, I will explain how to use this information to your advantage.

Building Your Brand on Twitter

Twitter is useful in building brand recognition and reputation. Since the service allows you to connect with the average person as well as experts, icons and even celebrities, you have access to a plethora of information, and with that, the opportunity to educate these people about yourself and/or your brand. With millions of accounts in the twitterverse, if you are not capitalizing on these chances and access to this information, it is a missed opportunity.

And though there are millions of Twitter users, many of them being company or business accounts, each and every strategy is different. Even those in the same niche will have a different style of messaging and implementation, as well as a different product. Though the target audience and demographic may be similar or even the exact same, the way you reach out to these people can be different.

When to Tweet

Once you have a decent amount of followers, it is important to find out when is the best time to tweet. With the website When to Tweet (www.whentotweet.com/), this information is easily accessible. The free account will analyze up to 500 followers and canvas each follower's last 200 tweets. With that information, the application will calculate the peak participation time. A pro account will analyze up to one million followers and 1,000 tweets per follower.

This information can vary depending on the location of your followers, taking time zones into account. Though you are not able to be monitoring Twitter at all times (everyone has to sleep!), you can set up automated tweets to fill in this time gap. This way your followers on the other side of the country, or the other side of the world even, will constantly be getting information. This tactic will depend on how big your brand is and how much of a following there is outside of the local area.

Messaging Strategy

Developing a messaging strategy is the most intimidating task of creating a Twitter strategy, as it is the most important. Your messaging tactics and techniques define how people will communicate with your company and your brand. There are many different approaches to Twitter messaging, but it all comes down to one thing: your goal.

What do you want to accomplish with your Twitter account? Are you only measuring number of followers? Are you monitoring engagement? Are you tracking the traffic to your website from your Twitter account? It is important to ask yourself these questions before developing a messaging strategy. You may be thinking, how do I decide what I really want to get out of this tool?

The answer to that question will be different for each company, depending on a number of variables. Does your company have a customer service issue? Then maybe using Twitter to connect personally with your customers is the most important to you. If so, you will want to measure your engagement closely. Does your company produce great content, but you have a feeling no one is seeing it? Then maybe measuring traffic from your Twitter account to your website is the metric you will be looking closely at. Basically, it depends on your company's wants and needs.

In order to get the conversation going, you should define your ideal Twitter follower, as you would define your ideal buyer or customer, as best as you can. Next, you need to research how that person acts on Twitter or social media sites in general. A very helpful tool is the techno graphic profile tool by Forrester (http://www.forrester.com/empowered/tool_consumer.html). This tool will tell you what type of social media consumer your target audience is, based on demographic information. This is extremely helpful in determining a Twitter messaging strategy, as you can then try to cater to the types of things your target audience will be drawn to. Here is an example, for a target market of 35-44-year-old men in the U.S.

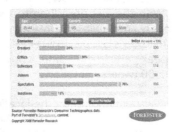

If you do not use the Groundswell tool, do your research via http://search.twitter.com/advanced. This free search mechanism is truly helpful in finding out information relative to Twitter specifically, rather than social media sites in general.

Next, you want to determine where social media fits into your Internet marketing plan as a whole. How will you be using your Twitter account? Will it solely be used for customer service issues? Are you looking at Twitter as a lead generator? Are you going to cross promote your other online efforts on Twitter? Determining what your Twitter profile will be used for is essential in your messaging strategy.

On Twitter you have the opportunity to connect with current and future customers, experts in your industry, news outlets, your own employees and many other businesses. There are a number of uses for Twitter, and there are ways to use your Twitter account for more than one effort. Twitter can be used for customer interaction, branding, public relations and search engine optimization, but it is a matter of determining the main use of your account and messaging accordingly.

Once you have researched your target audience and have fully optimized your Twitter profile through customization, you are ready to develop a messaging strategy for your account. It is important to remember that Twitter is only a channel to connect. It comes down to the techniques and tactics implemented to be successful. Before messaging, be sure a link to your Twitter account is linked everywhere your website is listed, for instance, on your website, your blog, your other social media profiles, etc. To streamline all of your social efforts, you must give access to these channels in every place a customer may stumble upon your business.

Remember: your tweets need to follow a certain motif, but still be different and diverse enough to keep people engaged. Your company messaging style will depend on your target audience, and like I mentioned earlier, every single messaging strategy is different. However, there are some tactics that have proven to be successful across all industries and audiences.

Popular and effective messaging techniques

- Connect your Twitter profile with another social site your company is active on, such as a Facebook profile, YouTube account or your blog.
- Plan to tweet a few very relevant pieces of information every day. When to tweet these resources will depend on the time your followers are most active. Since this may take a while to figure out (as you must build up a following to further investigate the best time to tweet), I suggest the morning.
- Promote the content you already have, and not just blog posts. Think about videos and webinars you have recorded previously. If you have a whitepaper or free guide that is a resource, make it known to your followers that it is available if they want it. What about fun photos of company events or happenings? You can tweet any type of content, and most publishers produce content daily. Let your followers know about it!
- Create fun content when you can. Having a holiday party? Is something funny or silly happening around the office? If so, take quick picture or video and tweet it! There are many applications that allow you to add photos and videos to your tweets very easily. I recommend us-

ing TwitPic (http://twitpic.com/) for photos and TwitVid (http://www. twitvid.com/) for videos. People enjoy fun and somewhat simple content sometimes, too. It also puts faces to your Twitter account. Show people that there are actual people behind your Twitter persona.

- Tag your tweets with a hashtag, or two. If you are in the Internet marketing industry, you may want to tag your tweet as #seotips or #socialmediatips. Even better, brand your tweets with a hashtag specifically for your brand. I.e. #vmtweets #vmtips #vmseotips are examples of hashtags I could use for Vertical Measures. By branding your hashtag, you are reinforcing your brand name, therefore promoting brand recognition.

- Ask questions. By asking questions, you are really encouraging interaction. And though most questions should be industry or brand specific, if it is a holiday or a certain day in history that everyone is talking about, address the occurrence but try to tie it back to your industry, if possible. By interacting with your followers about things other than straight business, it reminds people that there is an actual person behind the Twitter account.

- Encourage user-generated content (UGC). For instance, use the discussion you have on Twitter as blog posts. Tell your followers select tweets will be used on your blog, which will encourage more interaction and hopefully traffic to your blog. Use Twitter to encourage reviews of your company on Yelp.com or on your Google Places listing.

- If you have a special or a deal, promote it on Twitter. Go a step further, and promote UGC by asking followers to take a photo with the good, or something of that nature.

- Participate in popular Twitter hashtags, such as #followfriday or #ff, which happens every Friday. People tweet people they recommend others to follow, with the hashtag #ff or #followfriday. Use this tag to recognize people you have interacted with via Twitter or suggest Twitter accounts you deem influential. Try to provide some context with your #ff tweets, if possible. Though it is hard to provide context given only 140 characters, #ff is more useful with background information. You can find popular topics from Twitter's trending topics list, found on Twitter.com. You can set the trending topics to be geospecific, which is best if you are a local business, or worldwide.

- Host a live Twitter chat of some sort, specific to your industry. Popular chats are #seochat, #blogchat and #journchat. To do this, pick a day of the week or month where you will host a chat, asking industry-related questions of people following along. Some chats feature an expert in the industry and encourage others to comment on the answer to each question. Be sure to tag every tweet with your #chat hashtag, to make it easy for others to follow along, just by searching for the hashtag. Provide a full transcript of the conversation for interested parties after the chat ends, in case people missed something.

- Organize a tweetup. Tweetups are event that companies or groups of people hold to meet the people they talk to via Twitter, socialize and network. For example, the Phoenix Suns have a large Twitter following. Since 2008, the Suns have designated one home game a season as a tweetup. Twitter users who register for the event receive discounted tickets and credentials to attend a question and answer session with one of the players after the game. Attendants put their Twitter handle on their nametags so it is easy to meet others you converse with online, but may not know in real life. These events reinforce the community aspect Twitter brings to like-minded people, as engagement via Twitter happens whenever and wherever, and sometimes you never even meet people face to face.
- Host a contest. There are many ways to host a contest via Twitter. Be it answering a trivia question, answering an interview question, completing some sort of task (creating a video, writing a poem, etc.) or simply retweeting a message, there are some best practices to follow, as well as guidelines mandated by Twitter.com. First, offer a prize that is reasonable. Prizes can range from cash to scholarships to free services or goods. Your prize does not have to be outrageous to attract contestants, but it has to be something valuable. Before setting up your contest, read the guidelines to hosting a Twitter contest found here: http://support.twitter.com/entries/68877-guidelines-for-contests-on-twitter.

  **One thing NOT to do—sending contestants to your Facebook page and instructing them to "like" the page as entry into the contest. Facebook's contest guidelines are much stricter and they prohibit contests using the "like" button unless deemed acceptable through Facebook corporate.
- Apply calls to action to your tweets whenever possible. Encourage people to do something, rather than constantly pushing out information.
- Set up searches or streams for keywords or a set of keywords relevant to your industry. If people are asking questions and you have the answer, politely respond. If people are looking for resources and you have a blog post that is relevant, offer it as a resource. Make the first move toward interaction by giving people what they are looking for.
- Do not automate all of your tweets. If you are not going to interact on Twitter, why should others interact with you? Advanced Twitter users will be able to identify automated tweets, and if automation is your messaging tactic, you will not be successful.

Finding out what looks best for your brand may be a bit of a guesstimate at first, but as soon as you begin measuring engagement and conversations, you will see what works best for your brand.

Monitor the conversation

Once you start being active on Twitter, you should monitor conversations around your brand. Do this by setting up a stream in your account management program (TweetDeck, CoTweet, Hootsuite) for your brand name. This way you can see if people are talking about your brand even when they are not using your Twitter handle in the message. This is very important if you are using Twitter to deal with customer service issues.

Using Twitter as a Customer Service Channel

If you plan on using Twitter as a way to communicate with customers for customer service, it is important to do so in a professional way. Say someone tweets directly to you about a customer service issue. What should you do? You should have a protocol in place if you plan on dealing with customer service issues through social media, but some steps you may want to consider are as follows.

If someone expresses a customer service issue via Twitter:
1. Follow them. If you are not following them, they will not be able to direct message you. You will want to try to have the conversation privately, so direct messaging is the best option if you are discussing via Twitter.
2. Respond politely via @reply. Apologize for the inconvenience. Let them know you are aware that they are having a customer service issue, and tell them to direct message you. If they are not following you, you will not be able to DM them, so ask them to follow you for those purposes.
3. Once you are messaging privately, try to resolve, if possible in 140 characters. If the issue needs to be discussed at length, point the person to an e-mail address and assure the customer you will personally follow-up.
4. Once the problem is resolved (hopefully successfully), follow up with a personal tweet.

By making the first response public, it allows others to see that you are reachable via Twitter. Perhaps then more people will go directly to you to report problems, rather than posting a bad review on another website.

Many companies are already utilizing Twitter as a way to find and resolve customer service issues. For example, Best Buy created an entirely separate Twitter account dedicated to answer questions about their brand.[3] @Twelpforce, (www.twitter.com/twelpforce) is the "collective force of Best Buy technology pros offering tech advice in tweet form," according to the account's Twitter biography. What that means is, any Best Buy employee is able to register with the Twelpforce service using their employee identification and Twitter handle. Once registered, the employee is able to answer any question related to Best Buy on Twitter on the Twelpforce account. If they add the #Twelpforce hashtag to their tweet, their message will not only show up as coming from the @Twelpforce Twitter profile, but on a separate live stream (http://bbyconnect.appspot.com/), credited back to their original Twitter account as well.

By allowing employees' tweets to come from the company account when tending to customer service questions and issues, it gives the employee credibility. If someone asks a question about SEO on Twitter and I happen to see it, I may reach out to that person if I have the answer. But if I see the question in a search and the person I am responding to doesn't know who I am, they may take my reply with a grain of salt. However, if someone on the Vertical Measures account answered the same question, the person may take the answer more seriously, as the answer is coming from a reputable Internet marketing company.

Sniff out the Competition

There are many ways to spy on your competitors without them knowing a thing. We have already discussed setting up Twitter lists to spy on competitors, but there are other ways to measure your competitors' engagement and apply those findings to your own strategy.

Monitor Replies

In addition to setting up a list of competitors, set up a search for their username. This way you can monitor their @replies and see what people are saying about your competitors, be it good or bad. What questions are people asking? Is there sentiment positive or negative toward the competitor? To create this search in Twitter, search the username of your competitor and use the "Save this Search" option. If you are using a third party application, like Hootsuite, create the search as a new stream.

Take the information you find here and use it to your advantage. Is your competitor not taking the time to answer questions, but you have the correct response? What about if people are complaining about services or products from your competitor…can you offer something better? If so, you have the opportunity to swoop in on your competitors' customers, just by monitoring their brands on Twitter.

However, again a protocol is in order for these types of conversations. If you simply @reply with a sales pitch, people are more likely to think you are a spammer rather than consider your company as an alternative. Instead, try offering up simple advice or answers to questions and let the user decide.

Follow other social media sites

If your competitors are active on Twitter, most likely they are going to be active on other social media sites. Don't stop the stalking at Twitter! Find out how your competitors are interacting on Facebook, LinkedIn, YouTube, etc. If they include the social link to their Twitter account, most likely there will be links to other social sites.

This is a great way to evaluate what your company is doing, or not doing. Are your competitors engaged in interaction with people on a different network, like YouTube? If so, maybe you should consider getting a YouTube account or if you already have one, optimizing it to the fullest extent.

As well as checking up on their social media presence overall, be sure to keep up with their blog posts and articles. What type of content are they putting out? Are people responding to it (via comments, retweets or sharing in other places)? How are they promoting this content? Is the response positive or negative? The answers to these questions can provide insight when developing your own content marketing strategy.

Take a close look at their followers

By looking at your competitors' followers, you can determine the influential people in your industry who are on Twitter.

Tweepi (http://tweepi.com/geeky_follow/) will bring up an account's followers and sort them according to their followers' followers, who they are following, etc., and put the information in a graph:

Another service to look into is TwitterCounter (http://twittercounter.com/), which shows interesting metrics like the rate at which your competitor is following people, how often they tweet, etc.

This information will give you insight into your competitors' followers, but that doesn't mean you should go following everyone that is following them or even send messages to them. This information will help you gain insight into the people your competitor is interacting with.

SEO For Twitter

If you have a website, you understand how important search engine optimization is. It is as important to optimize your social media profiles as it is to optimize your website. Google now offers real-time search capabilities (http://www.google.com/realtime), which means it is indexing tweets and other data on the web all the time. As a result, you want to pay attention to your Twitter presence in terms of SEO.

Google has been indexing tweets and Twitter accounts for a while, so they do come up in regular search results. Take Vertical Measures, for example. Our Twitter account ranks sixth when you search Google for our brand name. Well-optimized Twitter profiles are prominently on the first page of brand-name searches in Google, so it is necessary to optimize your account for reputation management.

Provide the URL

Additionally, provide a call to action to your website visitors and ask them to follow you on Twitter, as well as other social sites you are active on. Make sure your Twitter account is accessible to visitors no matter what channel they are viewing your company on. Also, providing the link offers usability and will help drive traffic to your Twitter account, as well as up your Twitter account's rank in search engines.

The contents of your Tweet

When Google indexes tweets, the title tag (the HTML code that provides a title for the page) is about 65 characters long, which includes the account name and the beginning of the tweet. Therefore, your tweets should be keyword rich when possible. Obviously, don't stick keywords into tweets where they don't fit. But, when you can, start your tweet with the keyword that the post is about. Using industry buzzwords will put you in the position to make the most of real-time search capabilities. Provide your followers some context, as 140 characters sometimes just doesn't cut it.

Link back to your content whenever possible, but be sure to use a URL shortener like Bit.ly (http://bit.ly/), Ow.ly (http://ow.ly/url/shorten-url) or Google's own shortener (http://goo.gl/). These sites make your URL short enough to fit into a tweet, without taking up all your characters. Some shorteners, like Bit.ly, provide analytical data for your link, like how many times it was clicked, or track collective links (meaning if someone used their own short version of a URL, but it points to the same page), which can be beneficial when measuring your Twitter success.

Pay very close attention to the length of your tweets, especially if you are hoping to get retweeted. If your message is the full 140 characters, there is no way anyone will be able to retweet you without altering the tweet. Remember, when someone retweets you it is not only the amount of characters in the tweet itself, because "RT," @yourhandle and a colon are included. "RT @VerticalMeasure:" is a whole 20 characters extra. When you're dealing with 140 characters, 20 make a big difference. Keep that in mind when crafting tweets to allow room for retweeting,

Measuring Success

The ROI of Twitter

Twitter is a channel. It is a tool, and much like other tools, return on investment will not be able to be measured without a strategy in place where measurable goals have been established. If you have set up goals and are tracking links, traffic and even leads from Twitter, measuring the ROI will be easier. Without those goals in place, it will be very difficult to prove ROI from being active on Twitter. And the key to measurement is the goal, which should be established before a Twitter strategy is put into place.

Benchmarking

Before you start your social media marketing campaign, take benchmarks to know what the status of your company and website was at the beginning before you started your marketing push.

Benchmarks you should consider recording prior to a social media marketing campaign include:

- How many backlinks your site has
- How many people are participating in conversation on blog posts
- Which blog post has the most traffic
- How many visits your site gets
- Your site's bounce rate
- What keywords are drawing traffic to your site
- How many users subscribe to your RSS feed
- How many followers you have on Twitter
- How many Twitter lists you are listed on
- How many fans you have on Facebook
- How many followers are in your LinkedIn group
- How many people subscribe to your YouTube channel

In addition to the raw numbers, you can also benchmark things that aren't so much quantitative, but qualitative. These include:

- What is the general sentiment when people refer to your company?

- Are people eager to share your content?
- Is the conversation one sided?

Once you have established these benchmarks, you will have to decide what is most beneficial to the company to measure, because it will take an entire team to measure all of these metrics.

So, what can you measure specifically from Twitter usage?
- Followers (but remember, this is not a popularity contest)
- The rate at which you are gaining or losing followers
- Number of posts you have tweeted
- Your backlink profile
- Number of answers to a certain question
- Entrants in a contest
- How many times you are retweeted in a certain timeframe
- Overall replies in a timeframe
- How many customer service issues were talked about on Twitter
- What tweets caused the most attention
- What tweets caused people to unfollow you
- Overall sentiment to your tweets
- How many times a URL pushed out through Twitter is clicked on
- How much traffic came to your site through Twitter
- Your Klout score, which is your overall online influence indicator
- Your influence on Twitter

All of these are indicators to the success of your Twitter marketing strategy. Here is how to measure each.

Followers

As mentioned previously, TwitterCounter (http://twittercounter.com/) will provide insight into how many followers you have lost or gained in a certain period of time. It also forecasts how many followers you are expected to have by a certain date. Of course, you can also just compare your follower numbers on a weekly basis.

Tweets

- How many posts have you tweeted? Keep track each day of how many posts you put out, and compare it to the number of retweets and @replies.
- If you try a certain messaging strategy, like asking a question, track how many people actually engaged by looking at the @replies to that message.
- Investigate your backlink profile with Yahoo's Site Explorer (https://siteexplorer.search.yahoo.com/mysites) or with SEOmoz's Open Site

Explorer (http://www.seomoz.org/) to see who is linking to you. *But make sure you know how many links you started with!*

- If you have a contest where entrants must retweet something or include a certain hashtag, record how many people entered the contest,
- Track the URLs in your tweets. Many URL shorteners are set up to track how many times the URL has been clicked.
- Track how many times you are retweeted and pay attention to what is being retweeted. Are there certain types of posts that get retweeted more? If so, you could implement more of those types of posts into your messaging strategy. Check your retweet grade at Retweet Rank (http://www.retweetrank.com/). Retweet Rank represents the number of times a user has been retweeted by others recently.
- Track how many customer service questions, comments or complaints were brought up on Twitter.
- Determine what tweets caused the most attention by number of @ replies or track the URL in the tweet to see how many times it was clicked.
- Find out what tweets caused people to follow you or unfollow you, using TweetEffect (http://www.tweeteffect.com/). Just put in your username and the tool will output a chart that tells you the number of followers change (increase or decrease) after a certain tweet. People unfollowed after tweets highlighted red were posted, while people followed you after you posted tweets highlighted green.

Trend	Date	Update	Followers	Change
↓	Sun Nov 28 22:51:33	The local-search-marketing Daily is out! http://bit.ly/w82Gd9 • Top stories today by @smallbiztrends	2994	-1
⇧	Sun Nov 28 18:50:03	How Google's New Local SERP Affected Your Ranking - Posted by number1georgeThis post was originally in YOUmoz, and w... http://ht.ly /1ebVvF	2995	1
⇧	Sun Nov 28 00:33:24	The Vertical Measures Daily is out! http://bit.ly/9GgHdV • Top stories today by @weboptimiser_UK @lou1980 @soloparty	2994	3
↓	Sat Nov 27 20:31:19	The local-search-marketing Daily is out! http://bit.ly/a82Gd9 • Top stories today by @gsterling @smalbiztrends @localseoguide	2991	-2
⇧	Sat Nov 27 19:22:14	The link-building Daily is out! http://bit.ly/j • Top stories today by @wiep @cemper	2993	3
↓	Sat Nov 27 19:19:14	Homeland Security Seizes Control of Domains - Over the thanksgiving holiday the US Homeland Security Department seiz... http://ht.ly/1ebaXL	2991	-6
↓	Sat Nov 27 00:15:33	The local-search-marketing Daily is out! http://bit.ly/a82Gd9 • Top stories today by @ChuckReynolds @gsterling @smallbiztrends	2997	-1
⇧	Fri Nov 26 19:22:15	The link-building Daily is out! http://bit.ly/argy5j • Top stories today by @wiep @arloward @JulioJoyce @cemper	2996	2
⇧	Fri Nov 26 19:19:11	7 Non-SEO Tactics That Will Make You a Better SEO - Whiteboard Friday http://ht.ly/1eaDua	2996	2

Twitter in General

- Look at the overall sentiment of your social profiles. Social Mention (http://socialmention.com) will show you how much positive and negative sentiment is attached to your brand name across the web. Social mention also tells you your top keywords, top users, top hashtags and sources.
- Track how much traffic came to your site through Twitter via Google Analytics. If you do not have Google Analytics enabled on your web-

site, you should do so immediately. This free analytics program by Google allows you to see the back end analytics on your website whenever and wherever. With the Analytics suite, you can see where visitors are coming from, so you can see if people are finding your site from links posted in tweets. With Google Analytics enabled, you can see just how much traffic your Twitter profile is pushing to your site.

- Your Klout score is your overall online influence score, measured from 1 to 100. Your Klout score is measured with more than 35 variables between Facebook and Twitter to gauge certain metrics: true reach, amplification probability and network influence. True reach measures the size of the audience you are engaging. Amplification probability is calculated by how likely the content you tweet is acted upon. Your network influence is the level of the audience that engages you, based on how influential those tweeters are.[4] Find your Klout score by connecting your Twitter account to an application on www.klout.com. The tool will provide a summary of what each of your scores mean.

- Find out your influence specifically on Twitter with Twinfluence. (http://twinfluence.com/) by simply entering in your handle.

Where Are the Dollar Signs?

Okay, I know what you are thinking…"Here are many different ways to measure a variety of metrics on Twitter, but when are you going to tell me how much money I am going to make?"

I wish I could tell you that using Twitter account will increase your sales by 50 percent, but I can't. So how much money is Twitter going to make your company? It depends.

Though links lead to higher search engine rankings and generally higher search engine rankings lead to more traffic, more traffic doesn't always equal more sales. But if you build up your Twitter profile and have a good following and engagement level, you may see more traffic from Twitter. Traffic from Twitter is usually more qualified traffic; if people took the time to find your Twitter account and visit your website from there, they are already at least a bit interested in what you have to say. Qualified traffic can definitely equal more qualified leads or conversions.

Companies have reported increases in sales due to Twitter use. Dell, for example, has made more than $6.5 million from Twitter to date. Dell has been growing the Twitter following for its outlet store, @DellOutlet (www.twitter.com/dell-outlet), since 2008. Dell tracks its referral traffic, and can attribute referrals from Twitter to much of that $6.5 million[5]. Some people even first visited the Dell Outlet, but then proceeded to buy from the regular Dell store.

The ROI on Twitter in terms of dollars is very hard to pinpoint as it varies immensely depending on strategy and implementation, like many other marketing efforts. But the return on engagement can be plentiful—happy customers, who in turn spread the word about your business.

Other Uses of Twitter

Though many businesses and brands have adopted Twitter as a marketing and customer service channel, people use Twitter for many other reasons. Of course, Twitter is a very popular social network where people converse about, well, whatever they feel like.

Along with networking, another popular use for Twitter is job hunting. Like businesses, people build up their Twitter profiles to be authorities in their industries; experts on certain subjects and instead of marketing a brand, people use the channel to market themselves.

There are many recruiters active on Twitter, searching for job candidates. Also, many companies post job opportunities on Twitter, and often use the hashtag #job, along with the city the job is located in. In fact, I found my job at Vertical Measures through Twitter.

As a 2010 college graduate, I was very intimidated by my job search ahead. I networked in person and online, hoping to meet the latest and greatest people in industries that appealed to me. I ended up meeting a Vertical Measures employee at a networking event in fall 2009, and then followed her on Twitter for months, engaging whenever possible. In February, I found out about a scholarship contest Vertical Measures was hosting on Twitter. I entered and I won. When I picked up my scholarship, I got to meet the rest of the Vertical Measures team and began following all of them on social media sites—mostly on Twitter.

A few weeks before I graduated, Vertical Measures posted an internship opportunity on Twitter. I interviewed and got the position. After interning for about a month, a full-time position opened up, and I was hired. If I had not followed the company so closely on Twitter (and all of its employees, too) I would not have found out about any of the opportunities available.

In addition to being a great networking and job search channel, Twitter also has a way of bringing like-minded individuals together. As I previously mentioned, the Phoenix Suns possess a large Twitter following, and Suns fans converse about the games and players online by following Suns related hashtags. Often times, fans form online friendships without ever meeting in person, which is another way Twitter has affected me personally.

One of my favorite bands, Phish, has a very large fan base, many of which are active on Twitter. The band itself is not very active on Twitter, besides for updating set lists as shows go on, but the fans are, with or without the bands' involvement. After conversing with each other and following #phish hashtag conversations, Phish fan Steve Olker started the Phish Twibe.[6] A "Twibe" is just a group of people on Twitter who have the same interest, and anyone can start or join existing Twibes at http://www.twibes.com/.

The Phish Twibe grew to 386 members in 2010. Phish Twibe members host tweetups at every Phish show and constantly talk throughout the day on Twitter. The Phish Twibe took their group a step further by opening the lines of communication beyond 140 characters onto a message board and other social media sites, as sometimes Twitter conversations can be limiting. Thanks to the Phish Twibe, I have met many Phish fans from across the country and converse with people who share many of the same interests on a daily basis.

Many bands and musical artists have also begun to use Twitter as a way to directly connect with fans, offering exclusive contests and discounts through the channel. Likewise, Twitter is utilized by the news industry to break stories and give people the most up-to-date information available. News outlets have also used Twitter to find sources for stories and get feedback about certain issues—locally, nationally, and even internationally. Twitter is fast and far reaching, making it easier to connect with people anywhere and everywhere.

As you can see, Twitter is a tool that all different industries have adapted. Don't miss out on the conversation personally or corporately.

The Future of Twitter

Twitter Incorporated was only created in 2007. It is a relatively new tool, with much of its growth happening in the past two years. So where is Twitter going? Will it be around forever?

Many social networking sites have come and gone. MySpace was extremely popular in its heyday, but since Facebook came along, there has not been much buzz about it. So why is Twitter here to stay?

According to TechCrunch, Twitter had 75 million unique visitors in January 2010. In the month of January 2009, Twitter had about 6 million unique visitors. In one year, the number of unique visitors grew by 1,105 percent.[7] If that's not convincing enough, Twitter processes more than one billion tweets a month, according to research by PingDom.[8]

But it's more than just the amount of people using Twitter each day. Twitter has become part of peoples' routines. People have connected with celebrities—people who were somewhat untouchable before—through Twitter. People are hearing about news stories faster than ever. And who wants to give all of that up?

Also, businesses are finding ways to track sales from their Twitter efforts for relatively costs. More and more businesses are adopting Twitter as a way to track brand sentiment and solve customer service issues. Search engines are taking social cues into account when it comes to rankings, especially from Twitter. Also, Twitter itself is finally starting to monetize the network. People are posting groundbreaking news on Twitter before it is talked about elsewhere.

Take the top 10 most powerful tweets of 2010, for instance. People who work for Twitter picked 10 tweets that they felt showcased the year on Twitter, and the chosen posts truly illustrate the magnitude at which people are using and treating Twitter. The tweets included: the White House welcoming Russian President Medvedev to the social network; triathlete Leigh Fazzina tweeting for help when she crashed her bike in the woods; and reporter Ann Curry using a tweet to convince the U.S. Air Force to let a plane full of physicians from Doctors Without Borders land in Haiti after the massive earthquake in January 2010.[9]

Twitter has become a vehicle for advertising, marketing, friendship, connectivity and information in general. It has been life changing for some, and others have yet to discover its true value. But one thing is for sure, Twitter is not going anywhere. Jump on the bandwagon before it leaves you in the dust.

Endnotes

1   http://www.imoderate.com/main/newsID/50/do/press_release_Detail
2   http://searchengineland.com/what-social-signals-do-google-bing-really-count-55389
3   http://www.fastcompany.com/1648739/marketing-that-isn-t-marketing
4   http://klout.com/kscore
5   http://mashable.com/2010/01/14/money-on-twitter-dell/
6   http://blog.twibes.com/twitter-groups/phish-twitter-group
7   http://techcrunch.com/2010/02/16/twitter-75-million-people-january/
8   http://royal.pingdom.com/2010/02/10/twitter-now-more-than-1-billion-tweets-per-month/
9   http://yearinreview.twitter.com/powerful-tweets/

The Vertical Measures How-To Guide Series Available Now!

The Vertical Measures How-To Guide Series is for marketers, entrepreneur and executives that are ready to embrace emerging technologies that are taking businesses to the next level. The books highlight tactics that are worth focusing time and effort towards as well as those pointing out pitfalls to avoid.

The series provides deep insights into the world of emerging business technologies and covers topics including; Keyword Research, Facebook, Twitter, Local Search Marketing, Blogging and more.

- Succinct tactics for companies who are either using or plan to use new technologies to grow their business
- Written by industry experts with hands on experience in the field or discipline described
- Written specifically with the business and/or marketing user in mind –combining solid technical expertise with savvy advice.

Get discounted prices and take advantage of the opportunity to receive additional bonus materials for this series and other VM Press books like online at:
www.verticalmeasures.com/store/books